Richard Bailey

ISBN: 1519409532

ISBN 13: 9781519409539

Summary

In this modern world, where everything is calculated on computers and time is moving like a windstorm, people need recreational activities. Nightclubs and bars are the ultimate source of pleasure for nearly every age group.

The business of nightclubs and bars is very risky. Most bars fail within the first twelve months of opening because they don't have adequate plans in place. It is important to remember you are not just opening a bar but operating a business. The first priority is coming up with a concept for your bar; then, as with any business, you will require a business plan.

Chapter 1

The Nightclub and Bar Business Concept

What Are Nightclubs and Bars?

 The word *nightclub*, in its classic definition, conjures up an image of a swanky ballroom with an orchestra, perhaps a torch singer, and a wealthy clientele in tuxedos and evening gowns. In more modern times, however, the term is applied broadly to anyplace people go to drink and be entertained, be it a dance club, a rock music venue.

Live Music Venues: Many nightclubs base their business on big-name DJs; they each contain a bar, a floor, and a stage with a professional sound system. Some clubs book local talent exclusively, and some book mainly national acts.

Many clubs host a variety of genres, while others limit themselves to certain styles of music. Uniun Nightclub in Toronto, for example, caters to a wide variety of people, depending on the night that you attend.

Sports-Themed Nightclubs: Some nightclubs combine drinking and music with other recreational activities such as bowling, billiards, arcade games, skating, or ping pong. The chain Dave & Buster's has capitalized on this market, catering to adults who crave a drink as well as a diversion.

Comedy Clubs: There are two major types of comedy clubs: stand-up clubs and sketch comedy clubs. Both are commonly found in major cities but rarely elsewhere. Stand-up clubs usually feature a series of comedians performing short sets, followed by headliners who take the stage for a slightly longer time. Many clubs have two- or three-drink minimum requirements.

Sketch comedy clubs, such as Second City, host troupes of actors who put on short plays and improvisational sketches, during which audience members shout out suggestions that greatly influence the content of the performances.

Adult Clubs: Adult or strip clubs can be very lucrative; their stock in trade is the desire of men and women to watch dancers perform in varying degrees of undress. These clubs typically charge a cover (at least to men), and drink prices tend to run high.

Concert Nightclubs: Concert nightclubs feature live band music. Concert nightclubs are open only when there are shows going on. Some concert nightclubs are open to all ages; these clubs allow even patrons of nondrinking age to attend the parties. These types of nightclubs are not found often and are different from ordinary nightclubs.

Neighborhood Bars: Neighborhood bars can be found everywhere in the United States. Some of these pubs open as early as 6:00 a.m., and they sometimes close earlier than other bars, depending on their clienteles. These bars are perfect for small-scale entertainment options, such as darts, pool tables, video games, and jukeboxes.

Sports Bars: Depending on their capacity, sports bars can be specific versions of neighborhood taverns, or they can take on styles as big as those of clubs. Generally, sports bars offer some kind of menu options, such as sandwiches, burgers, pizza, sandwiches, and appetizers. Since the main attraction is sporting events, sports bars have televisions in view of every seat, sometimes all tuned to different channels. Audio and video technology come into play, with some owners spending a large percentage of their revenue on keeping up with the latest in technology, from satellites to big-screen TVs.

Brewpubs or Beer Bars: Microbrews are becoming more and more popular. In brewpubs, you can brew your own beer right on the premises. In beer bars, you can offer a large selection of different types of beer, including microbrews produced elsewhere. Most brewpubs only sell their own beer options on tap (draft beer), with a few selections of bottled, too.

Specialty Bars: Specialty bars, which concentrate on one type of libation, such as wine or martinis, or one theme, like cigar bars, are gaining popularity. Although some specialty bars focus on only one drink category, there must be a wide variety available within the genre. Take martinis: they have become very popular due to the variety they offer. The traditional martini still has a solid appeal if made with quality vodkas and gins, but other mixes, like sour apple martinis, have expanded the martini-drinking base, especially among women.

Clubs: Like neighborhood bars, nightclubs can take on a number of different personalities. A medium-size club might look like a neighborhood bar during the lunchtime hours, then spring to life with a popular band at night. Or, if you have a big enough budget, your club might be a large dance club where the most fashionable people and hippest celebrities hang out every weekend.

Chapter 2

Latest Nightclub and Bar Trends in 2016

Nightclubs have always had the same basic traits. They offer music, drink, and a good time. However, things change with the decades and even from year to year. What was hot one year might not be all that interesting any longer, and smart club owners want to know what is coming up and what they should offer to keep their customers happy and coming back for more. How drinks are served, how customers are treated, the environment, and other special touches are all changing with the times.

Keeping up with the trends is not always easy, but watching what customers want and how they behave can help. The top clubs usually set the trends, and those trickle down to others. Don't forget that even though trends come and go, some things remain the same. New drinks are always welcome, even though how they are served to the customer might change. Theme nights are always fashionable, but what those themes are drastically changes from year to year. Customers want to know what to expect, but they also want change. It can be hard to keep up, but it is certainly worth the time and energy for the success of any nightclub.

Portable bars: One trend of late is having bottle service at each table. This means customers might purchase a bottle of their favorite liquor for their table, and the drinks are mixed tableside. This means fewer trips to the bar less fighting for the bartender's attention for the customers, and more sales for the club. This might also mean staff has to keep a closer watch on customers who are too drunk to be served any longer, because they are pouring their own shots in some cases.

Specialty clubs: Some clubs are taking cues from the big ones in Las Vegas, Los Angeles, and New York. Swanky clubs have always been popular, but some are adding VIP rooms and tables for those who want speedy and personalized service. Staffs are equipped with headsets to communicate, and they try to anticipate the needs of the customers rather than waiting for them to ask for something. This helps to leave any customer with a feeling of special treatment. The right atmosphere and the right service can make all of the difference in retaining customers. Pool bars are very popular and are changing the shape of how people party. People begin partying in the early afternoon and end in the early evening. Patrons can now decide if they want to go out during the night or have an amazing day in the sun and get the same experience.

Art in the club: In this economy, fickle club-goers are demanding that their dollars go further, and entertainment is one way to offer greater value. We see more nightclubs incorporating live acts and finding unique ways to integrate entertainment into the venues. It seems natural that Las Vegas nightclubs are out in front of this trend. In Las Vegas, performance-driven DJs continue to pack crowds in every Saturday night. We also are seeing more artistically geared promotions as marketing directors come under increasing pressure to be creative in a hypercompetitive marketplace.

Social technology: Social media has taken over. A venue can become even busier during the night if people are tweeting, snap chatting, or on Instagram from the venue. Social media has become real-time marketing. For the patron who has not developed loyalty to a specific venue, it can draw that person to your venue.

Online booking facilities: Many nightclubs allow online booking of facilities, so people can book their arrivals and requirements ahead of time. These websites are user-friendly, and they can manage this system remotely from anywhere. The online scope of nightclubs is now growing, and club owners are now focusing on it.

Chapter 3

Elements and Concepts of Nightclubs and Bars

The following points are considered to be the elements of nightclubs. All the elements should be implemented to make a nightclub or bar successful. Although lots of books have been written on these subjects, in our research we are describing them in a brief manner.

Layout of the club: A growing number of nightclubs are targeting varied audiences, which requires different rooms and layouts in the clubs. Nightclubs can have elaborate dance floors in the center with DJ booths. Bottle service seating may also be provided, accommodating anywhere from ten to fifteen people per table, depending on the size of the club. Many clubs also offer private_party seating, such as cordoned-off VIP areas or private rooms, intended for special events. Nightclubs also have bars and dining room areas for those who prefer a more relaxing atmosphere.

Distinctive design features: The right d_cor spells the difference between a filled-to-the-brim nightspot and an empty one. The d_cor embodies the concept of the nightclub. It will set the tone of the club, the type of clientele it is after, and even the menu. A club decorated in mahogany and leather may be targeted _ upper-class patrons, while a mirror-and-smoke_designed club may be after the young, hip dance patrons. Many clubs are also going for the high-tech look with video screens, as well as state-of-the-art lighting and lasers (for example, Uniun Nightclub in Toronto).

Location: Location is crucial to the success of a nightclub. The club should be located in a place with significant numbers of potential patrons. A nightclub located alongside a church may attract a smaller clientele than one located alongside a hip bar. Also, check out the presence of competition in the area and whether the location will be able to absorb the addition of another nightclub.

A successful club is located where it is easily accessible and has plenty of parking for its patrons. What type of people do you want coming into your establishment? Is it the business crowd, who will stop for a drink after work and who need a quiet place to unwind? Then you will want to be located downtown in a central location. Do you want those who are going to stay for longer periods of time, who might want to listen to music at a piano bar, participate in a karaoke-type event, or just kick back and relax? Then a place in a strip mall or a small neighborhood business location would most likely be best. Perhaps you wish to have a place where there is lots of activity, such as dancing, pool tables, and shuffleboard available for your patrons; then you would want to look for a location that is easily accessible to major thoroughfares to draw large crowds of people. It will be important to determine what type of establishment you want and then design and decorate the interior to match the type of patrons you want to attract. No matter which you choose, having the proper ambiance will be important.

Club promoter: It's not an easy task being a club promoter; you have to be on top of your game all the time. You have to know what the up-and-coming music is and be naturally sociable, making everyone like you just by the way you speak and act. And knowing how to target your crowd in a nonspammy way definitely accounts for a lot.

When choosing a promoter to promote your bar or nightclub, you want to make sure you choose the one who best suits your venue. Check out other venues he or she has promoted in the past. Go to a local club night that he or she is promoting to make sure the crowd he or she is attracting fits in with your existing crowd. If you are opening a new nightclub, make sure this is the crowd you want. Most importantly, do not make a deal with a promoter who will make your club look busy while you are going broke. My rule of thumb is never to give a promoter a percentage of your sales. Give up door sales first. If you have to give up a percentage, never go above 10 percent.

Venue layout: This includes lighting, the placement of the DJ booth, and the size of dance floor. Is the space too dark? Too bright? Are there obstacles between the dance floor and the bar? All of these issues should be considered beforehand and dealt with by the club owner.

Disc jockey: A disc jockey (also known as a DJ or deejay) is a person who selects and plays recorded music for an audience. Originally, *disk* referred to phonograph records, while *disc* referred to compact discs; the latter has become the more common spelling. Today, the term includes all forms of music playback, no matter the medium. There are several types of disc jockeys. Radio DJs introduce and play music that is broadcast on AM, FM, shortwave, digital, or Internet radio stations. Club DJs select and play music in bars, nightclubs, and discothèques; at raves; and even in stadiums. Hip-hop disc jockeys select and play music using multiple turntables, often to back up one or more MCs, and they may also do turntable scratching to create percussive sounds. In reggae, the disc jockey_ or deejay_ is a vocalist who raps, "toasts," or chats over prerecorded rhythm tracks, while the individual choosing and playing the tracks is referred to as a selector.[1] Mobile DJs travel with portable sound systems and play recorded music at a variety of events.

The DJ and his or her ability to spin tracks can make the body shake uncontrollably in ways only music can. A DJ needs to read the crowd and anticipate what will make the crowd keep dancing. Make sure you choose a DJ who plays what the crowd wants, not what he or she wants to hear. The best DJs will play to the crowds and have the ability change their formats to cater to them. On another note, if you are trying to cater to a specific crowd, you might want to play a certain style of music that is enjoyable to that demographic, even though it might not be to another.

Sound system: How many times have you been to a large club where the sound was distorted and the music so unclear you couldn't understand the lyrics? It's no longer the eighties, so there is no excuse for that. A club needs to heavily invest in its sound system, as this is simply one of the most valuable components of their business.

Crowd: You can control the crowd you have if you properly focus your marketing and allow your venue's look, staff, and music format all to match. You will still have undesirable patrons coming to your venue, but dealing with them should be the job of your front door team. Proper training on how to talk to customers is key in these situations: "Make the customers love you when you are telling them no."

Exceptional service: Quality of service is a critical ingredient of every nightclub. Customers demand attention and friendly service, while feeling

---

[1] https://en.wikipedia.org/wiki/Disc_jockey#cite_note-0

safe and protected inside your premises. If you want your club to be known for the quality of its service, you need to have an adequate-to-high ratio of service personnel to customers (one service person to every thirty-five customers, or even fewer). You must also provide continuous training to your staff with regard to customer management and relationships.

Quality food: Food quality is also an important ingredient of the success of a nightclub. You can offer a simple menu with traditional bar appetizers, such as nachos or wings, while customers drink, dance, or simply enjoy themselves. Some nightclubs even go as far as offering food similar to that found in conventional dining establishments.

Entertainment and fun: Nightclubs have long been the purveyors of fun and entertainment in the evenings. The types of entertainment often provided by nightclubs include live bands, live national acts, DJs and MCs, theme-based parties, and at the lower end, jukebox and coin-operated systems. Entertainment may also include gaming facilities, such as pool tables, darts, video games, or pinball machines. Some nightclubs, particularly in Asian countries, even provide special rooms for karaoke singing.

Chapter 4

Nightclub and Bar Themes

Creating the right atmosphere for your nightclub is vital to achieving success. Patrons have numerous establishments to choose from when heading out for a night of drinking and dancing, so you must stand out from the crowd and demand patrons' attention if you want to be at the top of their lists. Many club owners debate whether to have a themed nightclub or big DJs week after week or to go with just some basic decor and focus on drink specials. To stand out and be noticed among the barrage of nightclubs out there today, look at your budget. A blend of all three ideas, based on your budget, might bring you the greatest success.

A theme can be anything, from a beach theme to a sports memorabilia theme to even a futuristic or space theme. The more unusual and different your theme is, the better. You want your club to be so unique that your patrons can't help talking about it at work on Monday. The best advertising in the world is free—word-of-mouth advertising—and the right theme can be just the thing to get people talking about your club all week long. Here are the few examples: If you give away a black tie for next week's black tie event when people are leaving your venue, people will think it such a different idea that people will talk about it and you may have even a higher attendance because of the word-of-mouth publicity.

Drink anywhere: People can have a drink just about anywhere. They can grab a bottle and head for their own living rooms if all they want is alcohol, but that is not why they go out to a nightclub. It is all about atmosphere. The whole point is to escape reality, forget about the bills and the problems, and just dissolve into a different world. A nightclub helps them take this fantasy to a whole new level and completely transports them to a whole new reality. Flashing lights, good music, good people, and some drinks—and life is good again.

Chapter 5

How to Choose the Right Name for Your Nightclub or Bar

A great name is the beginning of a great brand. Naming a bar calls for a large amount of creativity and planning. I mean, it's all about branding, right? Choose something catchy and unique. It should be memorable and create a certain feeling when heard. Here's a technique for creating one and making sure it's not already being used:

Brainstorm: Think about how you want people to feel when they hear the name. Write down the words on paper, and then categorize them by primary meaning.

Relate: Think about related words and phrases that evoke the feelings you want. Hit the thesaurus, and find all the synonyms for your words and phrases.

Relate more: Find out the Greek and Latin translations of your words. Figure out what colors, gemstones, plants, animals, and so forth relate to your words.

Experiment: Start playing with combinations of your various words and partial words. Don't be judgmental now—just make a list.

Reflect: Review your list, giving some thought to each name. How does it make you feel when you hear it?

Communicate: Go over the list with some people you trust. Have them tell you how each name makes them feel and how memorable they think it is.

Prioritize: Throw out any that just don't fit, and make a prioritized list of the rest.

Check trademarks: Make sure no one else in your line of business is using the names you're considering. You may still be able to use a name that's already being used by a completely different type of business, but be aware that it may create confusion for both you and the other establishment.

Check domain names: You want to make sure that an appropriate domain name is available. You want YourCompanyName.com, of course. If that's not available, you may want to reconsider.

Search the Internet: Even if no one has the domain you want, you still want to see what else is out there that has a similar name. That doesn't mean you can't use your chosen name even if you find something similar, but you need to know.

Check company names: If you're planning to incorporate, check with the secretary of state for the state you're incorporating in (or other appropriate office outside the United States).

Check assumed names: For sole proprietors, check for local assumed names (also known as DBAs). In the United States, you check this with the county clerk.

Stake your claim: Register your assumed name or file your incorporation papers right away. Also, start using either TM (trademark) or SM (service mark) with the name of your business. You do *not* have to register them to use them.

Get the domain(s): Find an inexpensive registrar and register your domain and any obvious variations on it. You shouldn't be paying more than ten dollars a year for each one, and at that price, it pays to prevent poachers.

Protect your brand: A US trademark or service mark costs $325.00. That's a drop in the bucket compared to what it will cost to defend your right to use the name later, but it's not really necessary for a small local business.

Tips to improve things:

1. Avoid generic names based on the names of people, such as Joe's Bar, Sam's Hardware, etc. They're not memorable and are nearly impossible to trademark.

2. Avoid generic names that describe the product or service literally. Generally, avoid geographical names. Besides not being very memorable, what happens if you decide to move or expand? The exception is if you're trying to create a strong local affinity—say, for a neighborhood bar.

3. It's preferable not to choose a name that might restrict future product or service lines. Be broad enough to include your wildest long-term vision for the business.

4. Try to keep the name short and easy to pronounce.

Chapter 6

How to Design a Logo for Your Nightclub or Bar

When you are opening a nightclub, image is everything. You want your logo to be cool and classy, maybe even a little elegant. Many nightclubs choose a minimalist effect for their logos, which prevents the logos from becoming outdated.

1. Make sure you have the right tools. In order to design a logo yourself, you will want to have the appropriate software, such as Adobe Photoshop or Illustrator.

2. Do some research. Take a look at club fliers for your area, or just walk down the street. You will be inspired if you just look around you. A minimalist look is always in style, allowing you to keep the same logo for years to come.

3. Choose your colors. Make sure you look at them printed out, so you know what they will really look like, because they will be different than what you see on a computer screen.

4. Get to work. Open a new file in your chosen software. If you are working in Illustrator, make sure that the logo is set to CMYK for four-color logos or that you have the appropriate PANTONE colors set up in your swatches palette.

5. Save your file, and submit it to the vendor of your choice. Make sure you convert all text to outlines and provide everything needed.

6. Start a contest, a Facebook page, and Twitter and Instagram accounts to start generating customer awareness of your new venue. These will also act as free promotions.

7. If all else fails, there are many businesses that design logos, and they will send you variations of different proofs, once you give them an idea of what you're looking for. 99designs.com has worked well for many people.

Chapter 7

Start-Up of a Nightclub or Bar

The start-up costs for a nightclub or bar include legal consultation and permit fees for a retail and food service establishment. Stationery costs include business cards, letterhead, and business brochures.

Insurance includes initial general and product liability premiums. You will need to cover one month's security deposit and two months' rent on the location to be allowed to build out the space before opening. (You will want to try to get a minimum of three to six months of free rent.) Start-up marketing covers the marketing campaign before launch. The website is a significant expense. It should offer basic information on the business, as well as a scalable social networking component: Twitter, Instagram, and Facebook.

How much does it cost to start a nightclub business? There are no hard and fast rules for setting the price tag of a nightclub or bar business. Your start-up costs will be influenced by the following factors:

- Size (seating capacity, dance floor area, etc.)
- Location
- Target market (Targeting college students will be cheaper than targeting celebrities and socialites)
- Type and features
- Concept and design of the establishment

Given the factors above, the price tag can be anywhere from $25,000 if you're buying an existing club to as much as several million dollars! The chart below estimates the potential range of start-up costs you might incur for your nightclub business. The actual cost may be lower or higher than these numbers, depending on the elements and features of your club. (Note that these numbers assume you will not incur the cost of constructing the nightclub building structure.)

ESTIMATED START-UP COST

Summary	Amount in $
Legal Help and Permits	18,000
Stationery etc	2,000
Insurance	500
Rent (security deposit & first month)	3,000
Start up Marketing	15,000
Website	25,750
Total Start-up Expenses	64,250
Cash Required	40,000
Other Current Assets	40,000
Long term Assets	95,000
Total Assets	175,000
Total Requirements	239,250

Detail	Low Range Amount in $	High Range Amount in $
Rent (security deposit & first month)	3,000	12,000
Leasehold improvements (heating/air conditioning, electrical, plumbing, painting, carpentry, kitchen upgrade, restroom upgrade, flooring, smoke detectors)	25,000	150,000
Interior Design and Refurbishing (including tables, chairs)	15,000	45,000
Equipment/Fixtures (audio/lighting lease payment, DJ sound system, bar equipment, lasers, smoke machines, stage sets, mirror objects, other equipment)	95,000	125,000
Kitchen Equipment (draft dispenser, microbrew equipment, commercial kitchen, hand sinks, concession equipment, etc.)	10,000	40,000
Cash Reserves	40,000	150,000
Signage (exterior, exit signs, etc.)	5,000	15,000
Legal Fees, Licenses and Permits	18,000	40,000
Point of Sales systems (including merchant accounts, credit card terminals, etc.)	10,000	35,000
Fire Fighting Enterprises (fire sprinkler systems, fire alarm, fire extinguishers, etc.)	15,000	30,000
Beginning Inventory (bar supplies, food)	15,000	40,000
Opening Salaries Deposits	15,000	50,000
Insurance	500	4,000
Grand Opening Marketing	15,000	25,000
Other Expenses (Add 10% of total)	22,150	76,100
TOTAL START-UP EXPENSE	239,250	837,100

The key is to research carefully the cost of the nightclub of your dreams. You may get to own a nightclub at far less than the low-end estimate, particularly if you are buying one from entrepreneurs in a hurry to sell it. Or you may start a nightclub from scratch and find that the required investment is much higher than the high-end estimate.

Chapter 8

Choosing Whether to Lease or Buy Your Nightclub or Bar

One of the main factors in deciding whether to lease or buy will be how much capital you have to spend up front. Your experience in the bar or nightclub trade can also be a big factor in your choice. It is often recommended to beginners in the trade that they start off by leasing their chosen business. That way, they don't risk any large sums of money and are able to pay smaller amounts on an ongoing basis to their landlords. Leasing is the easiest way to get into the trade, and it means you can budget your cost on a monthly basis.

When you lease, you sign a contract with your landlord for a specified amount of time—usually five years, although this can differ depending on the region you are in__and then you pay rent on a monthly basis.

You can also choose to lease the equipment you need inside your bar. This will enable you to build up an inventory as and when you need it in order to expand your business. If you choose to go this route, only get the essentials to begin with; you can add to these, if and when it becomes necessary. This is a good way to begin without having to spend large sums of money, but it will always prove more expensive in the long run than buying your own equipment. However, if you buy and then decide you want to change something (for instance, furniture, bar stools, etc.), you are stuck with what you have bought unless you want to make another cash outlay.

If you choose to buy your bar, then you purchase what is called the freehold property. This obviously involves a larger initial outlay, but you then own the bar outright. In the long run, this will turn out to be a cheaper option than leasing, but it all depends on your having the funds to front the purchase to begin with.

It is wise to consult a tax advisor to help you with the choice between leasing ___ buying. He or she will make you aware of the tax implications of both options and help you choose which is more advantageous to you.

Whichever option you choose, it is imperative that you hire a lawyer to look after the legal side of things.

Chapter 9

Licensing Requirements—United States

The licensing requirements vary from state to state in the Unites States and from province to province in Canada. Here are the general guidelines:

First of all, it is recommended that you form a corporate entity such as a corporation or an LLC (limited liability company), because your use of workers makes you an employer and thus subject to federal and state employment and unemployment taxes, as well as Medicare and social security taxes. With that in mind, you are required to obtain federal and state employment tax identification numbers, also called EINs. In addition, you will need to pay a business tax. The business tax, sometimes called a business occupational tax or a business license fee, is a flat tax usually paid annually.

Furthermore, your use of a trade name makes you subject to trade name registration. In the United States, a trade name is most commonly called a DBA, a fictitious business name, or an assumed business name. In short, you will need to register your trade business name with the state clerk, the county clerk, or the city clerk. When you get a federal tax ID number, use that instead of your social security number to open a bank account. Also, note that forming an LLC or incorporating will shield you from being held personally liable for debts you incur for the business and sign for as an officer of the corporation or LLC.

In short, file papers to incorporate or form an LLC, obtain federal and state tax ID numbers, and register your business or obtain a business license, and you will be ready to start your business.

Chapter 10

Decoration of a Nightclub or Bar

Lighting: Nightclubs frequently require jazzy, modern lighting and special effects, such as flashing lights of many colors, moving light beams, and smoke machines. Lighting is very important, because it can set the mood and tone for the moment or the night. When patrons enter a nightclub or bar at the beginning of the evening, the club should be a bit bright with warm colors, so the patron feels comfortable. As the night carries on, the nightclub will darken. Lighting on the dance floor and throughout the club can help energize the entire crowd in the room. If you are opening a big nightclub, it is important to have a good lighting technician who understands how to make the lights work with the music, so at times when the music is building up, the lighting is following the same pattern to create visually the same explosion that the music is creating with sound.

Decoration of the back bar: The back bar is a key component to a nightclub or bar. It gives the customers something to look at while they are waiting for drinks and adds d_cor to the entire venue. The back bar is where most of the plumbing and electricals are hidden, so you want to leave space available to access these things when it is time to repair them. Spacing of your back bar is crucial. You need to make sure all measurements are correct when you are fitting in items such as your sinks and beer fridges. Once your back bar is closed in with the correct measurements to fit everything in, you can start dressing it up to fit the theme or feel you want. Remember to use dimmers wherever possible, so that you can set the right mood, depending on the event or night you will be having.

Chapter 11

Marketing Your Nightclub or Bar

Marketing is the lifeblood of a nightclub business. If you expect five thousand customers at your door in one night, you need to find ways to promote your business, increase the level of awareness about your nightspot, and reach new customers while keeping the regulars.

Marketing research as a whole is outside the scope of this book. However, what follows is a list of factors that should be considered when conducting marketing research:

1. Environmental Analysis
   a. The Marketing Environment
      i. Competitive forces
      ii. Economic forces
      iii. Political forces
      iv. Legal and regulatory forces
      v. Technological forces
      vi. Sociocultural forces
   b. Target Markets
   c. Current Marketing Objectives and Performance
2. SWOT Analysis
3. Marketing Objectives
4. Market Strategies
   a. Target Market
   b. Target Mix
5. Market Implementation
6. Evaluation and Control

Some of the most common marketing strategies employed by nightclub owners include the following:

Advertising and promotions. Nightclub owners commonly use advertising to promote their businesses. Radio advertising has proven to be a potent tool for bringing customers to nightclubs, as has local newspaper advertising. If college students form a big part of your market, advertise in school publications (if allowed) or sponsor school radio programs. Brand awareness can also be enhanced with promotional materials (e.g., fliers and brochures) that can be distributed to patrons and radio listeners, among others.

Grand opening. Many new nightclub owners invest a significant portion of their marketing budgets in making a big splash with their opening events. The public relations activity as well as advertising work toward creating excitement about a new night spot. Some owners even sponsor contests on radio stations, giving away VIP passes in order to create awareness about their nightclubs. You will need to budget for a year of strong promotions at the start. Having a direct, consistent plan will help you stay on the right track. It will also allow you room for error, in case you have to change direction partway through.

Events marketing. Club events organized by themes have become essential marketing tools for nightclub facilities. Events typically bring the entertainment factor in a club up a notch, more so if an event features celebrities. Imagine the publicity your club will generate if you are able to bring in a major celebrity or any of the hip-hop royalty to attend your event! Your club can host large-scale indoor or outdoor events, frequent concert-style shows, product release parties, and so forth.

B2B marketing. If you are targeting travelers and businesspeople visiting the area, you need to have a presence where they go and stay. Travelers are often on the lookout for places to hang out at night to relax, unwind, and check out the hottest spots in the area. Reach marketing partnership deals with hotels so you can place your brochures in their lobbies, or better yet, in their guest rooms. Buy some ad space in airports.

Word of mouth. The hip factor, quality of service, and overall reputation of a nightclub can fuel positive word of mouth. Coupled with other marketing efforts, word of mouth is an essential crowd drawer in the nightclub business. For example, people are more willing to check out a club if it was highly recommended by their friends, peers, or relatives—even more so if word spreads that the club is where the hottest celebrities hang out at night.

Website. Your website is an integral element in nightclub marketing. A website can be an effective tool for raising awareness and catching attention. Make sure your site is listed in regional directories.

Chapter 12

What Makes a Nightclub or Bar Successful?

Everyone has his or her favorite bars, places where memories are made that last a lifetime. There is no common formula for what makes a great bar. A great bar is often born on its own, not made from a plan. What seems to be consistent is a passion for the project that is genuine. A bar owner who builds his or her vision will have a gathering place that people will enjoy for its honesty. Whether it is a passion for live music or for getting people together for the dance scene, building a place to support that vision will translate to popularity.

One key to a great bar is simply its physical presence. How the interior and exterior decor and the employees represent the establishment goes a long way toward its success. People who love where they work pass on that enthusiasm to patrons. It is much the same with the venue's appearance. The images, sights, and sounds all contribute to the experience. When they are consistent, the memories are stronger.

The type of bar does not matter as much as its authenticity. Having some sort of entertainment just to fill an evening will not raise a club's profile. Having live music because the owner loves it and wants to share it will contribute a lot to making the bar. A proprietor who loves to DJ will be able to put together a more authentic experience than one who just wants a DJ to attract a specific crowd. The same can be said for a karaoke bar. An owner or manager who is into it will organize it better from the heart than he or she would if it was just a side attraction.

An authentic experience will bring in patrons who really appreciate the venue, which contributes to the aura of a great bar. As word spreads from patrons to their friends, the community awareness of the bar will naturally expand. Buzz may be the most important factor in developing a cool bar. Once the type of crowd is established, others who want to be part of that crowd will naturally gravitate toward it.

There is no simple formula for creating a great bar. Anybody can put together any style of club he or she wants to, and all versions can succeed. Whether a corner bar, a sports bar, or a dance club, it can win recognition and build a long-term following. As long as there is a passion among the owners, management, and staff, everyone will benefit.

Chapter 13

Nightclub and Bar Security

Nightclubs are associated with the ideas of dancing, smoking tobacco, and dating. An inevitable result of those activities will most likely be quarrels and brawls among the customers. The goal of a bar, tavern, or nightclub is to provide a hospitable gathering place where patrons can have a good time listening to entertainment and/or dancing, while purchasing and consuming the establishment's primary product—alcoholic beverages. It is the last item, the consumption of alcoholic beverages, that tends to lessen or remove inhibitions in many people, which is the frequent cause of problems for a club's operators.

One result of such problems is increasing litigation against nightclubs and bars, frequently alleging excessive or inappropriate force used by staff or security personnel against patrons and/or a failure to protect innocent customers from assaults and injuries by others.

Because of their lack of prior problems or because of the types of individuals their atmosphere or entertainment attracts, such as older patrons, many taverns and bars don't use specifically designated or identifiable security personnel. Rather, they rely on their servers, bartenders, and management to handle any problems that may occasionally arise. And this is usually sufficient for them…unless their circumstances change.

Some establishments do, however, have a history of fights or violence. These taverns or clubs often cater to a younger, more risk-prone crowd. Trendy nightclubs, especially on weekends, may have long lines of young people eager to get into the current "hot spots." Some bars and nightclubs located near colleges and universities attract young (and often underage) people, who frequently engage in binge drinking or other risky behavior. The playing of pop music, especially by a live band or DJ, may also be a risk factor, since it often creates an atmosphere of intense physical activity, sometimes even reckless abandon. These establishments usually require security personnel and sometimes security equipment. At many urban nightclubs catering to young adult crowds, it is becoming increasingly common to use metal detectors at the doors to prevent the introduction of knives and guns, as some patrons seek to bring outside conflicts (and violence) into the clubs.

Some cities and counties now have laws or requirements as to what specific security measures bars and nightclubs must take. For the vast majority of cities and counties that do not mandate such measures, the national standard for the owners and operators is "reasonable care," based on the nature and location of each individual establishment and the specific risks each faces.

In each case, however, the establishment's management has a responsibility to use reasonable measures to provide a safe environment for its customers (invitees) and employees. That responsibility includes monitoring the club's parking lot and sometimes the sidewalks and other areas immediately adjacent to the building. These days, failing to warn of or protect customers from reasonably foreseeable violence, or the use of excessive or inappropriate force by employees to quell a disturbance or eject a customer, will most likely result in a lawsuit against the club and negative publicity. The following will help avoid that:

Nightclub concessionaires have found a way to resolve those problems: bouncers. *Doorman* and *bouncer* are informal terms for security guards employed at venues such as nightclubs to supply the security needs of the venues.

A doorman's primary duty is to prevent patrons under the legal drinking age and intoxicated, aggressive, or otherwise potentially troublemaking individuals from entering the nightclub. Doormen also use metal detectors to keep clients from bringing potentially hazardous and illegal items, such as weapons and drugs, into the nightclub. A secondary duty often includes the monitoring of clients' behavior to make sure that the nightclub's rules and alcohol regulations are followed. Also, doormen ensure that patrons do not damage the venue or the furnishings. In addition, doormen must resolve conflicts inside the nightclub, which may involve verbal warnings to rule breakers, forcefully separating individuals and groups, or making sure that trouble makers leave the venue.

Bouncers or doormen are also responsible for making sure entry fees are collected and verifying identification (especially with regard to the legal age of clients for alcohol consumption). On special occasions, doormen also escort and act as bodyguards for VIPs, employees, or female staff around the venue.

The increasing availability of affordable and reliable security and safety devices has created something new in these occupations over the years. Bouncers have made an increasing use of new device such as FRS radios, PMR446, and TETRA, also known as walkie-talkie equipment. Some venues equip their staff with Agent Radio Earpieces to stay in contact.

What's a bouncer supposed to do? A bouncer is the first person who makes contact with the patron.

The patron's first impression of the nightclub is formed then. The bouncer can be friendly and inviting, which will create a friendly ambience and an enjoyable night, or he or she can give the person a bad first impression of the bar by being terse or robotic.

The doormen are supposed to locate trouble before trouble appears. They have to prevent a problem from becoming a bigger issue. Doormen have to be ready and make sure their presence is very well known.

A vital aspect of this is projecting their voices and making eye contact. Most people would like not to fight with a giant bouncer. The bouncer only has to remind them of his or her presence, and they will think twice about their actions.

Size doesn't always work, however, and it is very important for a bouncer to know the correct technique of removing someone from the venue without killing, beating, or injuring that person.

There are many martial_arts techniques; however, a lot of them don't fit the job, such as tae_kwon_do, kung-fu, or karate. Judo lacks techniques for fighting with several opponents at once; ninjutsu lacks techniques for guarding a VIP. (Most ninja technique is based on evading, thus making the bouncer leave his primary task of defending the VIP, except from Koga Ryu Ninjitsu.)

Bouncers should know that a lot of brawls generate from a mixture of testosterone and alcohol, making the customer very emotional and crippling his or her sense of logic. One way to stop these troublemakers is to isolate the perpetrator from his or her companions. The bouncer will normally pull the perpetrator aside into a one-on-one situation and clarify, in a lucid voice, that he or she foresees no more trouble from the rowdy patron. This makes the situation safer for the bouncer and spares the person from embarrassment in front of others.

Bouncer equipment: Licensed security guards (guards who work for a security company, such as Skornik Security) usually carry handcuffs (in order to hold a perpetrator until the police arrive), pepper spray or gas guns, an expandable cudgel (baton), and an electrical paralyzer. All of this is usually carried in a tactical vest. Some nightclub security guards also wear bulletproof vests.

*

Chapter 14

Risk Management

Management decides what customers it will attract based on the club's location, the atmosphere and music format it provides, and its advertising. Promotions of two-for-one drinks; large, oversize drinks; or four-hour_long "happy hours" also set a tone and attract specific types of patrons. That tone will often determine what types of problems are likely to arise and what type and level of security should be provided. Management can, at any time, change that tone by changing the music, adding or changing the amount of the cover charge, increasing or relaxing the dress code, changing d_cor and lighting, increasing visible security, or taking other measures appropriate to that facility.

Nightclub owners should assess the risks to their establishments, including the crime history in their immediate neighborhoods and at any nearby bars or clubs. They should develop and have in place security plans based on the type of customers they attract and their known or likely problems. The plans don't have to be elaborate or even, in the case of small neighborhood-type establishments, written, although that is definitely preferred, but they should be thought through in advance. Once the potential problems and risks are identified, countermeasures can be developed and club personnel trained in their implementation. A security plan should be reviewed periodically (I recommend at least annually) to determine whether any changes have occurred in

Where security screening is used, that should take place immediately behind the doorperson, inside the exterior doors. A frisk is insufficient, as patrons are seldom, if ever, physically held or walk-through, depending on the volume of patrons) is recommended, along with training in its calibration and proper use. A female security officer is recommended as part of the team to frisk women who set off the metal detector.

Note that these two functions, doorperson and weapons screener, should be separate from any personnel used to collect money, check coats, or perform other functions at the door.

Bartenders and servers: The next line of defense for any establishment is its bartenders and servers. Each should be trained to identify patrons who are visibly becoming intoxicated, becoming loud and obnoxious, or looking for trouble. They should also be trained in basic nonconfrontational methods of cutting such people off from further drinking. Condoning the presence of visibly intoxicated persons, or turning them loose to drive on the streets, is a recipe for disaster and subsequent lawsuits. Training for these personnel should also include low-key behavior modification techniques that can often defuse a problem before it escalates.

Security personnel: The final lines of defense for most establishments are the inside security personnel or floor men, often referred to as bouncers. The term *bouncer* suggests an image of an untrained, physically large former football player or wrestler who handles drunk or unruly patrons by physically grabbing them and tossing them out the door. Unfortunately, this image is all too often real in some establishments. The actions of these untrained and often unscreened employees frequently give rise to subsequent injuries, deaths, lawsuits, negative publicity, and jeopardy to club licenses.

The true job of inside security personnel is to monitor the crowd to ensure that no one becomes unruly. *Deterrence and prevention first!* Patrons should be able to have a good time within established limits set by the club. To ensure this, security employees should be carefully screened for clear backgrounds, along with maturity and good judgment, and should have specific written guidelines for exactly what actions management wants them to take or not take. They should then be trained in those duties and their individual training documented. Their duties should be limited to security-type duties so that they do not become distracted or find themselves elsewhere emptying ashtrays or performing other nonsecurity duties when a problem arises.

One rule of thumb is that there should be one floor person for each anticipated fifty to seventy-five patrons, depending on the security history of the establishment. If unsure how many patrons are expected, management should base the number on the club's fire code capacity. It's always better to overstaff than to be caught short. On a heavy night, especially if there has been a history of problems in recent months or years, that ratio could be increased—for example, to approximately one floor person for every thirty-five anticipated patrons.

Sometimes club layouts require other inside security personnel to cover hallways, stairways, and entrances adjacent to men's and women's restrooms, where crowds may gather and trouble erupt. These personnel should be in addition to the one per fifty to seventy-five ratio used on the floor.

Management sets the tone and atmosphere of any club. Within that environment, floor people accomplish their jobs first by being highly visible to all present. They sometimes wear security-type uniforms or, as I recommend, brightly colored red or yellow shirts or jackets. Such shirts or jackets usually bear the words *Staff* or *Security* on the front and back in large white or black letters. In any case, they should be highly visible and not confused with any shirts or uniforms servers or other club personnel wear. A club might have its personnel wear tuxedos to raise the tone of the club and to assure they are visibly different from everyone else in the club. The highly visible presence of these floor men and women as they circulate throughout the club reminds patrons that their conduct is being scrutinized. In a large club that becomes crowded, security personnel should be in radio communication with one another, using radios with earphone extensions. One or more floor people in elevated "pulpits," often in the corners, can usually see over the heads of dancers and walkers and quickly identify disturbances.

If establishment rules are being violated, floor people or other employees should immediately and discreetly explain the rule to the violator(s) and then promptly *enforce* the rule. If possible, they should separate the violators from their friends so they won't become embarrassed. Don't wait, however, hoping the problem will go away. Again, good communication skills and tact are important when hiring floor men and women. Usually this warning is all that is needed to effect compliance. Other security personnel, servers, and management can be alerted to keep an eye on that particular person or party. Where an initial warning doesn't do the job, a second, less friendly but still courteous warning should be issued_ if not previously involved, management should be notified of the developing situation.

Removing _atrons: Sometimes visible presence, rule enforcement, and warnings aren't enough, and for the safety of staff and customers alike, an unruly patron must be ejected. Whenever possible, two or more security people should be present. (The rule of thumb is to have, if possible, at least one more security person present than the number of patrons being asked to leave_ but don't leave the rest of the club completely uncovered.)

Escorting a patron out of a club involves first explaining why the person is being asked to leave and then verbally requesting that he or she comply. If the customer has previously been warned, he or she already knows why he or she is being asked to leave, and, if treated courteously, may leave without a problem. If the customer hasn't been violent or overly aggressive and is not refusing to leave, he or she should be given a moment or two to collect him- or herself. Don't, however, permit continued drinking. Rushing things at this point can exacerbate the situation, as the customer tries to regain his or her dignity or self-esteem by demonstrating that "No one is going to throw me out!" An unnecessary fight frequently results.

When a cover charge has been collected for entry, a dispute sometimes arises with the patron(s) being ejected. It is usually wise to have management refund the cover charge in an effort to get the patron(s) to leave peacefully rather than risking a verbal confrontation that can quickly evolve into a physical fight and injuries, all over a few dollars.

In many cases, patrons being ejected are barred from returning for a set period of time or sometimes banned permanently. If the patrons have engaged in a physical fight or have resisted removal, I recommend they be permanently banned. If you don't ban them, and they return at some future time and cause damage or injury, your club will likely be sued.

Use of force: In escorting a patron out, blocking movements by the security officers using their bodies, and (if necessary) light touching to guide, direct, or even support an unsteady person may be permitted in some circumstances, but no greater force should be used except in self-defense or to protect some other person from injury or assault. Primary direction should be by verbal commands plus the presence of more security personnel than the number of people being removed. Absent a criminal act by the individuals being removed, grabbing them constitutes an assault and may result in criminal or civil liability to the club or security person. Verbal abuse of floor personnel or management by patrons is usually not against the law and should be considered part of the job. Physical force should never be used against a patron who has used only words. People's actions, not their words, are the key!

Only reasonable force__sufficient to hold or restrain an attacker or to overcome an attacker's use of force while defending others__is legally authorized in most jurisdictions. Such force should not be greater than the force being used by the attacker. The key word is *reasonable*, as in "reasonable to a judge or jury." Security officers or club personnel punching, kicking, tackling, dragging, and especially using strangleholds on patrons are almost always inappropriate and should be specifically prohibited by club management. Any greater force than the attacker is using could subject these personnel to criminal charges of assault and possibly civil charges against both the individuals and the establishment. Obviously, however, defending against a serious or deadly attack involving knives, guns, clubs, or other weapons is an exception to this rule, and security and other personnel should do what is reasonable to protect themselves and patrons from such assaults and to control the assailant(s).

When two patrons are being ejected for fighting with each other, the more aggressive patron should be ejected first. Only after he or she has been observed by security or management to physically leave the property, not just the building, should the second person be ejected, if possible through a separate door. Throwing both combatants out the same door together to let them "duke it out" is inappropriate and just asking for trouble.

When several persons are engaged in a fight, security and club personnel may have to peel them from the crowd one by one in an effort to break up the fight and escort them outside. The key is separating the combatants and then preventing those ejected from reentering the establishment or the fight. Where possible, one security person should remain outside or at the door and attempt to get ejected patrons to leave so that the fight does not resume or continue outside. In such a situation, the police should be called for assistance as early in the situation as possible.

It should go without saying that if a patron, even an intoxicated, obnoxious, and combative patron, is injured, he or she should be offered medical attention, usually by calling EMS or an ambulance. If the person is unconscious, medical help should always be called for him or her. Never eject a visibly injured person from an establishment without first offering to help that person obtain medical treatment. Even if the offer is rejected, it may still be appropriate to call EMS and let the injured patron personally decline medical services. This may be a case-by-case management decision or a policy set by management. A written report should be prepared in all such cases, especially if an injured person refuses medical attention.

If a patron refuses verbal requests or commands to leave after management has requested he or she leave or fails to promptly leave the property after exiting the club, in most states the person is guilty of criminal trespass. The individual should first be warned that the police will be called if he or she doesn't leave. If the patron doesn't then promptly leave, the police should be called. Also, if a patron physically resists removal, the police should be called and the patron removed and arrested. On-duty management, however, will have to make the decision to criminally prosecute the individual for trespass before the police are called.

Outside the club: Tavern- or club-operated parking lots should have a minimum of three foot-candles of lighting, measured horizontally at the surface throughout the lot. Security employees should monitor the parking lot(s), starting at least thirty minutes before closing time and continuing until all patrons and employees have left. This is especially critical if there have been prior incidents in the parking lot. Sometimes past activity will dictate that security monitor the parking lot(s) the entire time the club is open, either with one or more patrolling officers or through the use of continuously monitored closed-circuit television (CCTV) cameras. Incidents sometimes may erupt outside the club but still on the club's property. The visible presence of security may deter incidents from happening; if trouble is not deterred, security is then in a position to call the police and intervene as appropriate. If large numbers of patrons leaving at the same time have caused traffic or other problems for the police in the past, club management should contact and work with law enforcement to arrive at workable solutions to the problems. Management that fails to do so may incur the opposition, rather than the cooperation, of the police.

Conclusion: While lawsuits and bad publicity concerning security at nightclubs are on the rise throughout the country, they don't have to be. Establishments that use the guidelines described here can significantly reduce, if not totally eliminate, their exposure to such lawsuits and negative publicity. However, these guidelines and suggestions are not intended to provide the reader with a complete security program for his or her specific bar, tavern, or nightclub. Rather, they are a starting point and provide basic security considerations derived from what the author believes are well-accepted security principles and the best practices of numerous bars and clubs.

It should be remembered that all establishments differ in their size, layout, clientele, and specific risks, and that the clientele and risks may change over time, sometimes a very short time. Always consult with your attorney. Another good idea is to contact a professional security consultant for assistance in developing your establishment's security program.

Chapter 15

How to Make a Staff Loyal

Everyone finds value in him- or herself. Companies that have excelled teach their employees that people should be made to feel like they are winners.

Is your approach to your staff as positive as it can be? Do you give positive reinforcement, or do you remind your employees that they are not meeting goals?

Be supportive: People act in accordance with their images of themselves. If they see themselves as well regarded, they will live up to this standard. A supportive boss is important. Praise, appreciation, respect, new responsibilities, opportunities to learn, authority, and raises are rewards that play critical roles in your employees' self-esteem and productivity.

- People react negatively to attacks on their self-esteem as a means of self-defense and positively when given positive reinforcement. There is a difference between correcting someone and giving someone constructive criticism.

- People will surprise you if given the opportunity. Staff that you consider unwilling may emerge with fresh ideas.

- Make your expectations clear.

- Listen and hear suggestions.

Consider and reward new ideas: You will have some employees who cannot or will not respond to encouragement or suggestions. These people should not be exceptions. Goals are set for everyone.

Help your staff grow: Authoritarian management has gone by the wayside; newer generations coming into the workforce want to participate and have a say in their work environment.

If your employees learn one another's jobs, your personnel will have greater flexibility. There is room for growth for individuals, which creates a better sense of pride. Newer generations want to participate in meetings, and they want to be heard. Shared governance is a new management technique. Managers and staff share in decisions. Opportunity for input exists.

Increase responsibilities—learn to delegate: The manager should be kept in the loop at all times. This is sometimes a difficult thing for managers to delegate, but they need to learn that they can delegate and trust the people who work in their department.

Increasing the responsibilities of your staff will allow for more participation, and staff members will take ownership, resulting in job satisfaction and an increased sense of loyalty to your organization.

Giving people responsibility to do their jobs is hard for managers to do. Managers don't always delegate well; it is hard for them to let go. As a new manager, ten years ago, I was not able to delegate. It got to a point where I was not managing properly and not meeting my management role expectations. I had to delegate, or I would fail as a manager. I had to begin to pick people I could delegate to, and then I had to learn to trust. I learned to mentor, gave direction, and then allowed people to prove themselves. I had to accept that they would get to the same endpoint, but they might take different paths to get there. It was a strenuous learning process for me. Now I have supervisors that help me and report to me, and I could not manage without them. They are autonomous and have the authority along with the responsibility. I trust these people. They like their jobs and take great pride and ownership. Some managers are afraid of losing control. What is a manager's value if he or she cannot do a job?

Managers have a lot to gain from delegation. It takes away some responsibility, so the manager can do other tasks. At the same time, the manager gives employees the opportunity to grow and develop with new challenges. Employees become disgruntled and disinterested if they are not challenged.

There is excitement when someone is given new responsibility. Employee self-interest and goals will merge with the organizational goals, and then the employees find themselves participating in administrative decisions and processes that affect their daily work environment. They should be involved in the process.

Attitude: Managers need to set examples. Attitude is crucial. When the manager is negative, the staff can be negative. If the manager is stressed, he or she will stress the staff. I've had to learn to control my facial expressions. People can tell what type of mood I am in by the way I enter a room. Nonverbal cues are very strong. When you are a manager, you need to be able to present yourself in a professional, positive manner at all times.

Communication: Managers need to speak clearly, and they need to listen closely; they need to hear what the staff is telling them. There is nothing more frustrating for a staff member than to feel like he or she is "speaking to deaf ears." Communication is key.

When there are tough orders to carry out, you need to remind the staff that everyone is under the same pressure, including you and your boss. Manage up; don't put your boss down.

Increase your visibility: Show you are a team player and that you are willing to pull your weight and make sacrifices for the organization.

Be approachable and listen: Many managers are at a loss as to how to make employees more productive. Consider the value of a job. Where there are good jobs, there are workers. You want the best workers. In order to recruit and retain the best, you need to keep the employees happy.

It has been proven that most workers will leave their place of employment because of a supervisor. Be approachable and understand where the staff is coming from. Walk the talk. This will motivate the staff.

Recognition: Managers need to recognize and appreciate their staff. Positive reinforcement and public recognition are great ways to show employees you notice their efforts. The employee who does superior work will continue to work at this level when he or she knows it is noticed and appreciated.

Maintain your authority: While you are taking care of your employees and making them feel valued and appreciated, you need to maintain your authority. Show your employees that you are loyal to them, your boss, and the organization. If they see the boss has a vested interest in the workplace, they will feel confident in investing their time and energy as well. Show them that you support your boss, and you use your boss as a mentor.

Self-evaluation:

1. Are you approachable?

2. Do you listen and hear, or are you a manager who just runs around and doesn't really stay around for outcomes?

3. Do you really care about your employees?

4. Evaluate your relationships with the people you work with.

5. How do they view you?

6. Are you open with the people who report to you?

7. Do you give feedback for their ideas after you ask them for participation and suggestions?

8. Are you open minded?

9. Do you try their suggestions or just push them aside?

You need to have an open door policy. Encourage people to come to you. This may take time, as they need to learn to trust you. Be honest with the people who work with you. I always feel it is better to say someone works *with* you instead of *for* you. I always find a team approach is better.

Conclusion:

In conclusion, these are just some things you can do to create a superior and loyal staff.

Make people feel like they are appreciated and valued.

Work with them and credit them for what they do.

Participate in staff appreciation activities.

The most important thing I feel a manager can do to recruit and retain a loyal and motivated staff is just to treat them the way you would like to be treated. I promise, you will be successful. You are only as successful as the people who work with you!

Chapter 16

Bringing It Together

This book touches on some great aspects of the nightclub and bar business. It is important to make sure you have the necessary money to fund your project, remember to stick with your vision and give it the right amount of time for it to develop. Having a good team that you can depend on from top to bottom will help increase your chances of success. Remember to treat your staff the way you would like to be treated. It is just that simple.

www.ingramcontent.com/pod-product-compliance
Lightning Source LLC
Chambersburg PA
CBHW071549170526
45166CB00004B/1608